I0087797

# CAREER BOOK 1

### 17 Career-readiness Strategies
### for Parents
### of Elementary School Students
### With Special Needs

JIM HASSE

# DEDICATION

To my sister, Mary,
who is my model for how to use soft skills effectively
in achieving corporate goals.

# CONTENTS

# ACKNOWLEDGMENTS

A special thank you to Peter Altschul, Fernando Botelho, Earl Brancel, Judy Ettinger, Floyd Harris, Pam Hasse, Nan Hawthorne, Mary Krohn, Nancy O'Connell, Liz Seger, Ruth-Ellen Simmonds, Don Storhoff, Mårten Tegnestam and Bob Williams – all of whom (among many others) have provided me with valuable guidance during critical moments in my career development.

# WHAT I BELIEVE

Over the last 20 years, I have identified a range of time-tested strategies I believe parents can use to prepare youngsters with disabilities for the world of work.

I believe guiding parents in implementing these strategies on a wide scale will bring these two results:

- More people with disabilities will be ready for work.

- Employers will find more job candidates with disabilities who they consider qualified for open jobs.

That's why I seek non-profit and corporate partners which have wide, established connections with parents who are looking for the answers I can provide about how to help their youngsters with special needs prepare for meaningful careers.

My message: I believe people can put disability to work as a competitive edge in today's job market.

For a long time, those of us dealing with disability employment issues have realized that individuals with a disability can add a valuable perspective to corporate efforts in the mainstream business world.

That message has had a difficult time getting public attention, but that may be changing.

I believe we can now more confidently state this finding: Employees with disabilities are more likely to bring drive, focus and innovation to the workplace than their non-disabled counterparts.

Consider the following three contemporary authors who have recently brought those three "advantages" of disability employment to the public's attention through books which have received good reviews in the mainstream media.

**First**, in "The Triple Package: What Really Determines Success" (2014), Amy Chua and Jed Rubenfeld discuss the reasons behind personal achievement.

Successful people, they say, tend to feel simultaneously inadequate and superior. They:

1. Believe they are, in some ways, exceptional.

2. Are insecure about their worth or place in society – that they're not "good enough."

3. Resist the temptation to give up instead of persevering in the face of difficult circumstances.

They may appear to have a chip on their shoulders because they have a need to prove themselves.

For those of us with a disability, for instance, we may have a personal need to prove to others that we are the "exception" to commonly held beliefs within our society about people with disabilities in general.

I believe that inadequate/superior package tends to generate a personal drive in "overachieving" individuals with a disability – a need to prove oneself by sacrificing present gratification in pursuit of future attainment.

I must confess that this inadequate/superior duality fits me to a tee. For a thorough examination of that duality in me, go to the directory for my series of seven Amazon books about my personal transformation stories as a person with cerebral palsy at cerebral-palsy-career-builders.com/transformation-stories.html.

**Second**, Geoff Colvin sums up the power of deliberate practice with a purpose in his book, "Talent Is Overrated: What Really Separates World-Class Performers from Everybody Else" (2010). He writes:

> "...The most important effect of practice in great performers is that it takes them beyond -- or, more precisely, around – the limitations most of us think of as critical."

He pinpoints exactly why I believe it makes good business sense to hire people with disabilities who have developed the motivation to work hard at precisely the things they need to improve so they can contribute to a company's bottom line.

Colvin cites research that indicates what we think of as "innate talent" is more accurately termed "long-term, sustained practice at what really counts" driven by a passion to reach a goal (or in response to the triple package described above by Amy Chua and Jed Rubenfeld). In other words, Colvin says it's all about self-discipline no matter what the motivation.

**Third**, in "David and Goliath: Underdogs, Misfits and the Art of Battling Giants" (2013), Malcolm Gladwell offers a new interpretation of what it means to live well with a disability.

His main point: What is innovative, beautiful and important in the world often arises from what looks like suffering and adversity.

In other words, being an underdog can change people. "It can open doors and create opportunities and educate and enlighten and make possible what otherwise may seem unthinkable," Gladwell writes.

Gladwell even promotes the idea of a "desirable difficulty," such as dyslexia, a learning disability that causes much frustration for students as they learn how to read but, at the same time, forces them to compensate for that barrier by developing better listening and problem-solving skills – and by being innovative.

I encourage you, as a parent, to keep these considerations in mind as you help your youngster with special needs prepare for a meaningful job in an integrated work situation.

I researched and wrote the material for this book long before the afore-mentioned authors became popular. Over the last 20 years, I have gradually realized the importance of disability as the foundation for the resiliency of humankind throughout history.

However, only in the last five years have I publicly admitted that my disabilities, while they have made life tougher for me to live, have also, within certain contexts, become an aggregate advantage for me.

That reconciliation – and even love – of one's personal vulnerabilities perhaps come with age and the advantage of hindsight.

At any rate, please keep these initial remarks in mind as you review the following career-readiness strategies for your youngster. Your youngster's personal circumstances as well as the National Career Development Guidelines in the back of this book can also temper your thoughts.

Will your youngster be able to frame disability in such a way when he or she makes the transition from school to work that will help hiring managers recognize disability's competitive advantage?

Will those hiring managers seize the opportunity they have for boosting drive, focus and innovation in their workplaces by hiring your son or daughter?

I believe the answer to both of those questions can be "yes."

But, first things first. Your youngster needs to first grow in self-confidence.

# STRATEGY 1 – LEARN WHAT IT MEANS TO WORK

I first learned about occupations and job titles when I began attending orthopedic school in second grade. I remember the big black locomotive spewing black smoke and the black dust from the adjacent coal yard.

I had also learned that the guy in bib overalls peering out the window of that locomotive was a "locomotive engineer."

As a farm kid, I had not seen a locomotive before and couldn't identify a picture of it when I first entered orthopedic school during an IQ test (to the chagrin of my new teacher), but my mom countered, "What do you expect? He's a kid from a rural area."

I knew what a carpenter was, though. My great grandfather always had a hammer in his overalls and was the fix-it person around the farm. One day my grandmother asked me what I wanted to be when I grew up, and I replied, "Carpenter."

Keeping in mind my cerebral palsy, she scoffed, much to my disappointment and confusion. "You better think of something else," she replied sharply.

What I didn't articulate at the time and she didn't understand is that I wanted to be a "builder."

But, by the time I was 10, I had a pretty good feel for what people did for a living and what job titles were all about.

And, I knew I wanted to build things through writing.

I loved to write, but it was not easy for me. It was a grind.

It helped to have a good mentor at home, though. My mom wrote "how to" articles as a hobby, and, as a "retired " teacher, she was teaching me how to write -- first poetry, then Haiku, then short stories, then essays and then term papers.

## My Five Families

My "first" family consisted of dairy farmers. My mom, dad and two younger brothers and sister all helped doing the daily chores. I even washed the evening dinner dishes while the other members of the family were working in the barn with our 60 registered Brown Swiss cows.

But, then came grade school, and, over a span of seven years, I lived with four different "house families" during the week. That was necessary because I attended an orthopedic grade school 60 miles from our home farm.

During my *first* "house family" experience, I lived with a middle-aged couple with a grown family where the father was a custodian at a state university, and the mother was a homemaker.

The father in my *second* "house family" was a factory worker. He made Oscar Mayer wieners. The mother stayed home, helping raise two grade-school boys.

My *third* "house family" had two pre-school children. Both the mom and dad were educated as teachers. The father worked as an accountant and built the family's home, including a "secret" fall-out shelter (yes, it was the 1950s).

In my *fourth* family, I joined two daughters and a brother, all in grade school. The mother was trained as a dental hygienist and the father was a professor of agriculture who managed a university experimental farm. I still remember the day he received his master's degree.

So, by the time I was in eighth grade, I had experienced family life under five very different circumstances. I knew I had career choices beyond dairy farming, which I knew I couldn't very well do anyway due to my disability.

What I didn't know at the time is that I would eventually become a company journalist (circa 1960), business communicator (circa

1980), and online content developer (circa 2000) -- all job titles that not yet been "invented" in 1953.

But, by eighth grade, I knew what various jobs meant in terms of every-day living. And, I knew I wanted to be a writer or more specifically, a journalist.

It's never too early to begin talking to your youngster about interests and the specific jobs and job titles which are associated with those interests. At the elementary level, career information for kids usually focuses on:

- The awareness of individual differences and preferences.

- The enjoyment of learning and doing.

- The skills to make a decision.

- The broad characteristics and expectations of work.

# STRATEGY 2 – NURTURE SELF-ESTEEM

Dr. Carolyn Myss says self-esteem isn't something your youngster is born with; the ability to "manage feelings" is something he or she acquires through nurturing people such as yourself -- through your youngster's environment and experiences in life.

That's good news because it shows how important your role as parent, mentor or coach is in shaping that supportive environment for your youngster, especially in the elementary grades.

According to Nathaniel Branden, author of "The Six Pillars of Self-esteem" (Batam Books, 1994), self-esteem has two interrelated components.

One is the sense of basic confidence in the face of life's challenges (dealing effectively with cerebral palsy, for instance). The other is a sense of being worthy of happiness (possessing self-respect).

For your youngster at the elementary level, both components of self-esteem can perhaps be best understood as the ability to "manage your feelings."

Learning how to manage your feelings about yourself is the key to self-esteem, the point at which you say to yourself, "I can do it" and "I'm worthy of happiness."

Branden summarizes his six pillars of self-esteem like this:

- **Living consciously:** being aware of what you're doing while you're doing it.

- **Self-acceptance:** owning the truths regarding your thoughts, emotions, and behaviors; being kind toward yourself with respect to them; and being "for" yourself in a basic sense.

- **Self-responsibility:** owning your actions and owning your capacity to be the cause of the effects you desire.

- **Self-assertiveness:** treating your needs and interests with respect and expressing them in appropriate ways.

- **Living purposefully:** formulating goals and establishing and implementing action plans to achieve them.

- **Personal integrity:** maintaining alignment between your behaviors and convictions.

That may seem heavy, but Branden is basically saying environment can influence self-esteem, but self-esteem also relies upon how your youngster reacts internally to that environment.

Branden points out that those who have learned how to "manage feelings" (having a level of self-respect) will have the capacity to respect others. Individuals with healthy senses of self-esteem, he says, do not seek to prove their worth by trying to make others appear to be wrong. They are not belligerent.

But, youngsters (and people of all ages) with poor self-esteem often belittle themselves or their own comments when communicating with others. They'll say things such as, "I think..." or "I feel..." but then apologize for expressing a new idea or concept.

Or, they'll make self-deprecating remarks about themselves, such as, "Oh, I'm so stupid..." at doing something or when they make a mistake.

They'll put themselves down. They'll laugh at inappropriate times. They'll make statements into questions by raising their tone of voice at the end of a sentence.

Those with a disability may also play "the victim" and look for and subsequently find offense almost everywhere when there is none intended.

## Provide an empowering environment

You can empower your youngster by providing an empowering home life (or frequent place to visit, if your situation is not home-based) which is, in itself, a career builder. It's a career builder because it fosters self-esteem development -- a place where managing your personal feelings is the norm.

In such an environment, individuals relate to one another at a high level of consciousness, self-acceptance (and acceptance of others), self-responsibility, self-assertiveness (and respect for the assertiveness of others), purposefulness, and personal integrity.

That type of gathering place offers your youngster an opportunity to develop, even at an early age, a healthy sense of self-esteem. To do so, however, such an environment needs to offer your youngster an opportunity to:

- **Feel safe,** secure in the knowing that he or she will not be ridiculed, demeaned, humiliated or punished for openness and honesty or admitting, " I made a mistake…" or "I feel down right now…"

- **Feel accepted** and treated with courtesy; that means being listened to, invited to express thoughts and feelings, and being dealt with as an individual whose dignity is important.

- **Feel challenge** by learning new things which excite, inspire, test and stretch both ability and imagination.

- **Feel recognized,** acknowledged for personal talents and achievements which are based on reality instead of paternalism.

- **Receive constructive, unfettered feedback** as a means for improving performance in non-demeaning ways that stress positives instead of negatives and that concentrate on building up personal strengths.

- **See that innovation can be exciting**, and, as a result, personal opinions are solicited and valued.

- **Gain easy access to information** and resources about careers and about what makes work valuable and personally rewarding both from an abstract and general standpoint as well from the perspective of family members and friends.

- **Gain appropriate authority** to take initiative, make decisions, and exercise judgment in school matters which involve career development and vocational training.

- **Live under clear-cut and non-contradictory rules** and guidelines which provide a structure so he or she knows what the family expects from each of its members on a day-to-day basis.

- **Feel empowered** to solve as many problems as possible on a personal basis instead of passing responsibility for solutions to other family members.

- **See the rewards for success** are far greater than any downside for failure so that appropriate risk taking becomes a family norm.

- **Learn and be rewarded for learning** that expands knowledge and skills.

- **Experience congruence** between values and actions within the family, so, as integrity is exemplified by each member, there is a motivation to match what all family members see in each other.

- **Experience being treated fairly** and justly so that the family becomes a rational, trustworthy unit for everyone involved.

- **Perceive that personal work done** within the family is genuinely useful and worth doing.

Within that type of family unit, Branden says, your elementary-school youngster will learn how to manage his or her feelings in appropriate ways and, in the process, realize a higher sense of self-esteem in terms of effectiveness ("I can do it") and self-respect ("I'm worthy of happiness").

For youngsters with a disability, that growth in self-esteem is a career builder which is often a critical factor in how effective they are in developing a meaningful career and an independent, fulfilling life.

# STRATEGY 3 – ADDRESS FEAR

How to manage fear is a challenge your elementary student with special needs is probably facing, even though you may not recognize it at first as a parent, mentor or coach.

If I had to select one word which describes what it's like to grow up with a lifelong disability such as CP, it would be "fear."

However, I remember my dad saying he was shy as a kid but that he gradually grew out of it. So, I'm not sure if my insecurity is in my gene pool, in how I was raised or in how I personally reacted to my disability.

For years, I held my fear inside, and, when I was about 10 years old, I truly felt I was psychologically unstable because I didn't how to manage fear and I never discussed it openly with my parents.

I told no one that I feared I was psychologically unstable because I was afraid a good deal of the time when I was outside my "safe" environment (i.e. home). My insecurity was producing a fear that something was "wrong" with me because I was afraid once outside our home environment.

Here are snippets of my mother's published writings between 1956 and 1958 about how we both grew in self-confidence (she as a mother and I as a child) through my summer camp experiences.

> "… I was the mother of one of those wonderful but baffling noisemakers called a boy. Jim seemed well-rounded and secure as long as he was at home. The moment he was taken

away to visit or found himself involved in a party, he became oversensitive, shy, and cowered at the sight of strangers. The halo he wore so well at home slipped when he was exposed to the social side. He became weepy, unsure, and just wanted to go home.

"In spite of all of our efforts, I could see that Jim was growing ill at ease among people. Even though he was involved in a classroom situation within a "special" school for children with disabilities, he was missing out on the social side of school.

"We had to face it. In spite of having frequent, small groups of guests in our home, our seven-year-old was not becoming socially adapted.

"So we sent him to camp …

"Through our Easter Seals clinic, we arranged to have Jim spend a two-week period at Camp Wawbeek, Wisconsin Dells, WI.

"… When I looked ahead at the two weeks of camp life for Jim, I wondered how I would survive without him during that period. Then I realized my greatest fault. I had a tendency to become over-protective. I was molly-coddling Jim into fearsome insecurity. Jim was becoming the person who might have trouble adjusting to the hard world. I had to do it – send him to camp.

"… Camp experience proved to be stimulating for both of us. Sometimes parents are so close to their child that they cannot see him. To get an overall picture of your child and his challenges, you must get away."

60 years later, these are the highlights I now recall from my camping experience:

- **Disability culture:** One of our camp counselors helped us discuss whether we liked being called, "handicapped." We found ourselves brainstorming about alternative terms after learning about the historical context of "handicapped."

- **Gratitude:** I learned how to write a "thank you" note to my sponsor.

- **Expanded interests:** In addition to pool time, picnics and hikes, I dabbled in ceramics and photography – activities not available at home or school.

- **Acceptance:** My roommate, who also had CP, believed in flying saucers (which I thought was a little strange). But he became my best buddy outside of grade school.

- **Freedom:** I felt free for the first to function within an accepting community without the stigma of being disabled or the structured routine of the classroom.

- **Conflict resolution:** While working on the camp's newsletter when I was 15, I had to handle an accusation from a fellow volunteer that "I was not pulling my weight."

I now believe my 10 years of camping experience between 1950 and 1960 turned out to be key stepping stones on my way to a meaningful career.

Perhaps sharing my personal story with your youngster would be helpful in at least opening a conversation with him or her about how to manage fear.

Try to find ways your youngster can express his or her feelings of insecurity – through drawing, diaries, play acting, casual chats etc. The key here is to let him or her know that learning how to manage fear is part of the journey in "growing up." It should not evoke shame, quilt or punishment.

## My Struggles

As a child, I feared being left by my parents with others -- even with a familiar baby sitter.

I remember the panic I felt one evening when I was left in a church pew alone because my parents temporarily stepped out of the sanctuary.

In grade school, I feared walking down the aisle of any public forum (movie theatre, church, school etc.) because I would picture myself falling in front of the crowd due to my stiff legs and the pitiful stares I would get from onlookers because of my disability.

In high school, I clung to the hallway lockers for fear I would be trampled by the bigger, more "normal" students, especially the guys in black leather jackets and ducktails. I also had an aversion to three-foot wastebaskets because one time a fellow student (a hefty Wisconsin farm girl) had to fish me out of one. I had grabbed it for balance and, instead, flew head first (and arms) into the trash.

The summer before my first year in college, I silently cried in the back seat during a family car trip out West when my mom reminded me that my first college classes started in just three weeks. I knew I wasn't ready to face that new environment, and I dreaded even thinking about it during a carefree (and safe) summer vacation.

During college, I settled into a comfortable routine but worried about how I would fare after graduation when I would enter the rough and tumble "real world." Real-world business people, I thought, would hear my slurred speech and immediately discount my intelligence and training. And, I wouldn't be able to get a job.

But, for me, failure, at that point, was not an option. In my experience, there was no advantage to failure. By growing up on a farm, I knew what a crop failure meant: less feed, less milk, less income, less freedom.

As a young person with a disability, I needed to earn an income to become independent -- to be the first in our family to get a non-farm job. Yet, once on the job, I feared being suffocated in unchallenging work within a "going nowhere" company in a back-water rural area.

## Success and Recognition Helped Me

But, by the time I became 30 years old, I began to realize some success (and recognition by others) in my work as a corporate communicator, and that helped me learn how to manage my fear.

I found that people generally don't think much about what makes others "different" because they are often preoccupied with their own concerns. And, I learned that organizations, especially my employer, tend to change through one "pocket" at a time instead of top down (at the leadership of the CEO, for instance).

Now that I look back on my career, my "false" fears of failure may have actually crippled my growth. Yet, on the other hand, I'm probably stronger now because I experienced that struggle.

We are crippled by false fears when we experience failure in advance of its actually happening (and that failure may never happen), according to Seth Goden, whose latest book, "Poke the Box," is a call to act on personal initiatives.

Goden says leaders tend to be more fearless than their followers. Followers, heeding the voices in their heads, tend to believe there is no advantage to failure, and, as a result, are stuck in old behavior patterns. Leaders, on the other hand, understand that learning comes from failure.

"Nobody is successful all the time, and fear is not productive. You need to show up again and again and keep playing the game," emphasizes Goden, who has had 13 books on the New York Times "Best Seller" list. He says his first book, by the way, was rejected by 900 publishers.

## Successful 20 Percent of the Time

Goden explains that a person is usually successful 20 percent of the time in any endeavor. "Keep track of your chances," he recommends. "Your next effort may be the time you'll be in the 20-percent category."

That's one challenge I'd recommend passing along to your youngster: How to manage fear by anticipating that he or she is right now within the 20-percent range of success (after so many unsuccessful attempts).

Goden notes the job market has changed. "There are no more paper-shuffling jobs that pay $150,000 a year," he says. "Obedient cogs (in the wheel) are being replaced by individuals who are willing to be accountable and to face failure and to take an entrepreneurial approach to work. They are innovative and willing to take risks."

What really resonates with me is Goden's admonishment to "believe in your ability to shine a light for people and share what you know that is beneficial to others." The key, he points out, is accumulating ideas, beliefs and information that stand out from the crowd and people find useful.

The workarounds for fear (which are actually methods for how to manage fear) that I have developed for myself over the years turn out to be a response to that charge. I have learned how to be an innovator and a delegator.

As an innovator, I noticed that people within my workplace were often more intrigued by my creativity, even though my ideas may have turned out to be half-baked and not workable at all. At least, they saw that I was thinking -- and thinking in terms of the company's success. Once the company's bottom line became the focus, my disability (and my timidity) seemed to disappear.

For instance, I worked for a dairy processing cooperative which manufactured commodity cheese in bulk for major food companies. As an upstart during the early 1980s, I found myself asking why, as a highly regarded cheese manufacturer, we should not tap into the value-added portion of the cheese business by developing our own brand and marketing channels so our dairy farmer members could reap increased returns from the milk they produced.

And, as a member of senior management during the 1990s, I was plugging away at the same "value-added" orientation -- only this time as the point person for the organization's strategic planning process.

We were still in the commodity cheese business, but we had developed a whole new value-added product offering: whey products for pharmaceuticals, bakeries, infant formula etc.

In short, I found my disability didn't much matter, if I shifted the focus to innovation. Creativity trumped my disability and deflected any concerns my colleagues may have had about it. And, that made it easier for me.

As I assumed more responsibility and moved into senior management, I also learned how to delegate hands-on work -- especially work that was difficult for me because of my disability.

I started hiring high school students for after-school jobs and then began to offer paid internships for college students. As the organization and my responsibilities grew, I eventually developed a team of five people, each of whom had authority to carry out specific duties (and get the recognition for it).

Over a 28-year span, I hired, trained and developed more than 25 people in the field of corporate communication, public relations and member relations. And, I learned to welcome failure in myself and others because it helped our team grow.

My lack of knowledge about how to manage fear and my fear of what could happen (and often doesn't) because of my disability have gradually disappeared.

# STRATEGY 4 – MANAGE MOTIVATION

Michele Shusterman is founder of cpdailyliving.com and parent of a daughter who is in elementary school and has CP.

Michelle writes on her site's inspiration page:

"As we have gotten to know and understand Maya (alongside her disability) we have learned that she tests us like any other child. She makes it her business to try and tug at our heart strings just to see what can happen. We would be in big trouble now if we had let that pouty lip of hers determine what she could and couldn't do."

I remember when my own mom would leave me lay in bed at five years old in the morning instead of quickly and easily dressing me herself. Instead, she would wait to see how long it would take until I decided to dress myself (which I could -- with some effort on my part).

She knew I could do it. I was just relying too much on her because it was an easy way out of a "daily chore" I dreaded. But, that was my first taste of discipline that I vividly recall. My mom rescued me from "learned helplessness" long before the term became common in academic circles for the trap motivated moms with a child who has a disability need to avoid.

Yes, motivated moms also need motivated kids.

Motivated kids thrive on encouragement, love, learning and conversation with you, as a career-coaching parent. Those positive experiences are especially important for your elementary student with special needs.

# My Little Successes

During my early grades, my mom seemed like she was always helping me prepare for the day when I could live an independent life. In fact, as I look back, I can trace my "entrepreneurial spirit" back to her tutorage. I remember her helping me:

- **Plan** and plant an herb garden every year while I was in grade school so I could give not-so-common herbs to my school teachers, neighbors, house parents etc. every holiday season.

- **Make** a variety of reed baskets by soaking the reeds in our upstairs bathtub and turning the bathroom into a mini-manufacturing room from which I gave (and sometimes sold) examples of my handiwork.

- **Learn** photography and the difference between a photo essay and photo story through my photography project in 4-H.

Those little successes (which I still vividly recall six decades later) gave me the motivation to eventually tackle the mainstream job market and start my own business, even though I had CP.

Motivated kids have an internal desire or need that energizes their lives and gives them direction. Many people believe that personal drive is more important than natural ability or aptitude. But, no one has really discovered how an individual acquires personal motivation, writes Geoff Colvin in his book, "Talent Is Overrated: What Really Separates World-Class Performers from Everybody Else" (Penguin Group, 2010).

State of Oregon school psychologists admit that, at some point in your youngster's development, you will probably feel that your youngster lacks sufficient motivation. Most parents face this worry that their son or daughter kid is not motivated.

Different "signs" may trigger this concern. Your youngster may seem turned off by everything, may complain excessively about school or home life, may drop out of activities, or act particularly bored with routine and non-routine events.

It's important not to react in ways that might actually make the problem worse. After all, encouragement, not criticism, inspires us all, particularly motivated kids. When you criticize (even constructively), your youngster is often discouraged and less motivated to do what is expected.

To this day, I remember my mom saying," You're not doing well today with your speech," because I internalized what I took as criticism. I have difficulty recalling when she said, "You're speech was particularly clear today."

## When Motivated Kids Do Well

On the other hand, by noticing and encouraging good behavior, youngsters typically repeat that good behavior. Motivated kids feel good about themselves, their behaviors improve as the improvements are recognized, and their motivation increases.

All motivational problems are not simply solved, of course, and can require professional help. But, you, as a career-coaching parent, can make a huge impact by focusing on and supporting what your youngster does well.

In addition to providing encouragement, parents of motivated kids who do well in elementary school or outside activities tend to:

- **Show** love by providing support for their youngsters as they develop their interests.

- **Teach** responsibility by acknowledging positive behavior in completing chores, completing homework and participating in social activities.

- **Be** a role model by valuing education, exhibiting family values and modeling expected behavior.

- **Provide** a range of experiences through sports, music, volunteer activities, and travel so youngsters discover and develop their strengths, bolster their self-confidence and acquire the motivation to do more.

- **Talk** to their youngsters about activities, schoolwork, friends, and interests as well as listen as they discuss these topics.

- **Be** aware of potential issues by recognizing the general problems and pressures their youngsters may face (and need help with) while dealing with the challenges of growing up.

Of course, growing up with a disability means your youngster will probably face a whole range of other challenges specific to his or her special needs.

So, cultivating an open dialogue about those specific issues and how to resolve them as well as about general "growing up" questions can often be critical in determining how effectively your youngster makes the transition into adulthood.

# STRATEGY 5 – VALUE PATIENCE

We're not very patient in the U.S., and that has served us well in many cases for more than 200 years. As Americans, we pride ourselves as innovators, particularly when it comes to quick fixes.

But, our lack of patience and a short-term focus is perhaps becoming a detriment to our businesses, our economy and our globe. In short, we may be short-changing ourselves.

Here's part of a comment Veronica posted in one of my online forums in October 2010:

> "Most managers are looking for what someone can do for them right now, and asking them to look down the road a year is beyond the skill set of most company managers in the U.S. In Asian companies, that is another matter. And that is why we have many Asian companies outperforming their U.S.-based counterparts."

I'm convinced that, if we're going to adequately address some of our long-term problems in this world, we need to place a greater value on patience as a key ingredient in a good skill set and on a long-term focus in the political leaders we choose, the job candidates we hire and the business people we promote to higher positions of authority.

Eye-popping breakthroughs in medicine, energy, and agriculture seem to be making headlines at a more frequent rate than ever before. Those breakthroughs will be creating new and exciting jobs during the next decades that we now can't even describe.

Those who have learned patience (particularly patience developed within a good skill set through personal struggle to reach a long-term goal at an early age) may be just the right people for those positions -- jobs your elementary student with special needs could perhaps someday hold.

To qualify for those jobs, he or she needs a good skill set built on a foundation of patience and a long-term focus (exactly the attributes dealing with special needs tends to foster).

# STRATEGY 6 – USE VISUAL LEARNING

Lise LeBlanc is a coach and consultant for Connexions Vie-Travail, Moncton, New Brunswick, Canada. She has developed an exercise that has been helpful for me (even as a 71-year-old).

LaBlanc developed "Handy Tips" to help her clients identify their personal strengths, choose personal-experience stories to illustrate those strengths and anchor those strengths to their fingertips so they are easily accessible and memorable.

This may seem like a "grown-up" exercise to help clients increase their confidence during a job search, but I see value in it for your elementary youngster also because it so visual and basic.

Here's how to make this "handy tips" activity work for your youngster. All you need is some unlined paper and colored crayons (5 different colors).

- **Give** your youngster a sheet of unlined paper.

- **Instruct** your youngster to trace his or her dominant hand with the non-dominant hand. This activates the left and right hemispheres of the brain.

- **Help** your youngster to identify five key strengths he or she has to offer at home, in school, in family recreational activities outside the home etc. (strengths that are valued in our culture and in workplaces).

- **Help** your youngster write down one or two words per finger (the first things that come to mind).

- **Have** your youngster pick five crayons (five different colors), one for each finger. Help draw or paint each finger in a different color. How this is done does not matter as long as five colors are used. Give time here. Do not rush. The objective is to integrate the positive words/attributes and to associate them with a color.

- **Ask** your youngster to think of specific supporting stories where the word/attribute was demonstrated fully and completely. For each finger, your youngster needs to identify one or two stories. Once a story is identified, your youngster can write a few memory jogger words at the tip of the finger - - as though the hand had rays of sunshine coming out of each finger.

- **"Talk out the hand."** That means asking your youngster to present his or her hand to you or another person. With the hand map in front of him or her, your youngster can present one finger at a time with the supporting story.

  During the time your youngster is talking about the strength and its attributed story, he or she can apply light pressure at the tip of that finger. This is called anchoring.

  Once your youngster finishes talking about the finger, they then go to the next and continue. You simply need to listen and not interrupt (non-verbal encouragements such as smiling and nodding are allowed).

This visual learning exercise builds self-confidence in your youngster by identifying in concrete terms what she or he is "good at doing." It also is good practice for eventually identifying strengths as a job seeker.

That strength identification is sound preparation for developing a resume, and the storytelling practice is an excellent foundation for doing well in job interviews once your youngster enters the job market.

# STRATEGY 7 – LEARN
# VIRTUAL TEAM-BUILDING SKILLS

In 1994, when I was 51, I bought my first home computer when I decided to quit my corporate job and start my own business. I had a "dumb" computer terminal at work for about 10 years before that, and I had to take crash courses about how to use Windows, correspond by e-mail and "surf" the Web to get up to speed as a "virtual entrepreneur."

Virtual learning, though, was only a vague concept to me two decades ago. I had not heard of "instant messaging." But I was intrigued by Mosaic, the forerunner of Netscape.

Fast forward to 2004. With the help of many people throughout the world, I had been developing web site content for seven years. One of my clients eventually became my full-time employer, even though it was located in Manhattan, New York City, 1,000 miles from my small home town in Wisconsin.

As a telecommuter between 1999 and 2009, I worked as a member (and full-time employee) of a small but dedicated "virtual team" of eSight Careers Network freelancers, contractors and full-time employees scattered throughout six states and two provinces of Canada. We used e-mail, instant messaging, and telephone to communicate with each other.

Essentially, we were all involved in virtual learning – finding what worked and didn't work as a virtual team in building eSight Careers

Network, a cross-disability community for exploring disability employment issues.

It's a leap many people have taken during the last two decades. Our world entered the cyberspace age, and virtual learning became possible.

So, I now believe tapping current virtual learning opportunities while your youngster with special needs is still in elementary school may eventually give him or her a "leg up" in tomorrow's job market.

## Today's Learning

There's a lesson I've learned by going through this experience -- just one slice of my career. Formal education can't be expected to prepare you for a job; it can only show your youngster how to absorb knowledge and learn the skills he or she will need once in the job market.

Because of my experience with virtual learning, I've done a complete 180-degree turn about the role of education in my life.

In 1965, I believed the key role of higher education was to prepare me for a job (a concept many liberal arts campuses didn't appreciate back then).

Today, I believe the key role of higher education is to show us how to learn throughout our careers (a concept many on campus have forgotten in the current push to prepare students for the work world).

We may have forgotten that the knowledge we learn in the classroom today may be outdated or not relevant for us tomorrow. That is certainly true for the elementary student you're currently mentoring.

## Preparing for Tomorrow's Learning

So, how do you help your youngster prepare for such opportunities?

Samuel Beckett wrote these 12 words I believe are worth remembering:

"Ever tried? Ever failed? No matter. Try Again. Fail again. Fail better."

Could it be that formal education will give your youngster a greater capacity to "fail better" at what he or she learns while working in tomorrow's business world?

We can only imagine what working will be like when your elementary youngster enters the job market 15 years from now. There will certainly be new occupations and new job titles with yet-known qualifications.

So, I believe a wise use of your time right now in mentoring your elementary student is to focus on developing, over time, his or her ability to use today's virtual learning opportunities for:

- **Niche Networking** – developing contacts worldwide within your youngster's age group who have similar interests, traits, goals, dreams etc.

- **Global skill building** – developing basic interpersonal communication and teamwork skills which cross national boundaries and cultures.

- **Experiential learning** – developing the ability to apply personal attributes in learning new skills through trial and error (by simply doing an interesting project, for instance, in which success or failure is not a primary concern).

## A Virtual Game

Here's a game that you may want to reconfigure to fit the current ability and needs of your elementary school youngster.

- **Begin** a virtual team-building session with simulated face-to-face interaction via webcam on a laptop, iPad etc., involving yourself and your youngster or one of your youngster's friends or schoolmates.

- **Select** an age-appropriate game, such as Scrabble, for the two to play, either as a one-session event or an on-going competition in which each player is virtually notified that "it's your turn."

Take time to chat with your youngster what he or she likes or dislikes about interacting with another person online. What is good about it? What are the barriers compared to face-to-face interaction over a simple game?

You'll both be establishing a foundation for wisely choosing more advanced virtual learning opportunities as your youngster matures.

# STRATEGY 8 – START CARER PLANNING NOW

Career planning is not answering the question, "What do I want to be when I grow up?" Instead, career planning:

- Is a lifelong process.

- Involves using a set of career planning skills that must be learned.

- Helps organize thinking about one's education, work, and other life roles.

- Is proactive even in the face of unplanned events.

According to mychildsfuture.org, a career planning checklist needs to answer these questions:

- Who am I?

- Where am I going?

- How do I get there?

- What are my next steps?

- Where am I now?

With each change within your youngster's development, help him or her return to these five questions and make sure goals and action plans are on target.

One of the simplest ways to organize a career planning checklist is to focus on these three elements:

- Self-knowledge

- Knowledge of the world of work and education

- Decision making and goal setting

## Self-knowledge

Help your youngster understand his or her unique qualities. That goes a long way in answering the first career planning question, "Who am I?"

Interests, values, skills, personality type, and career beliefs are the personal characteristics most frequently discussed by career professionals.

Be aware of these markers of self-esteem and talk about them with your child at the earliest age. Ask the right questions (not "What do you want to be when you grow up?") – something, instead, like this:

- "What are your dreams?"

- "Why do you like to do that?"

- "What do you feel you are good at?"

- "What is important to you?

Helping your youngster along this discovery process can be a part of your everyday conversations with him or her. Casual conversations at the spur of the moment often reveal insights that can become part of career planning.

## Knowledge of the World of Work and Education

You can help your youngster learn about what is "out there" in terms of occupations by following up on natural curiosity. Observing everyday life in your home and community offers many chances to think about how people and the work they do affect their lives.

As your youngster expresses an interest in an activity, person, or product, take the opportunity to explore:

- **What** are those people doing and why?

- **Where** did that product come from, how was it made, and who made it?

- **What** does that type of person actually do in his or her job?

Tying your youngster's understanding of the world of work to education is also critical. Kids need to connect what they are learning in school to their dreams. So, extend your conversations and observations this way:

- **Are** those workers using math (or writing, speaking, science, history) to do their jobs?

- **How** did that person prepare to do that work?

- **What** kind of school or training would I need to do that?

- **What** would I have to do to go to that school or training program?

In some situations, you may not know the answers to these questions. No one, not even career development professionals, know everything about work and school. Take advantage of this opening to work together to research the answers and open up more possibilities.

## Decision making and goal setting

Self-knowledge and knowledge about work and education are meaningless without the next step: making decisions based on that knowledge – decisions which present themselves later than at the elementary level.

In middle school, for example, your youngster may choose which career paths to explore as part of a curriculum. In high school, he or she are deciding which classes to take, what to do after they graduate, and where to look for work. As adults, your son or daughter will also make career decisions regularly (when, for example, to take additional skill training or request a promotion).

So, that's the big picture when it comes to developing a career planning checklist with your youngster who has special needs. Between the ages of four and 10, your son or daughter will likely form a lasting impression of what life is all about and how he she can fit into it from an occupational standpoint.

It's a developmental stage when you can influence how that picture takes shape by introducing concepts which can later add up to a robust career plan.

# STRATEGY 9 – FOSTER
# SEVEN CAREER DEVELOPMENT SKILLS

The Research Institute has identified a total of 40 developmental assets which form a foundation of behaviors that propel elementary students toward a meaningful career as an adult.

Those 40 assets, based on extensive review of the theory, research and practice by the Research Institute, are positive experiences and qualities that help influence choices young people make and help them become caring, responsible, successful adults. See www.search-institute.org/research/developmental-assets.

After reviewing those 40 assets, I've selected seven of them which, based on my personal experience, I consider key career development skills for your elementary school youngster.

## First: Parent Involvement in School

This means, as a parent or other mentor, you are actively involved in helping your youngster succeed in school.

As a school teacher in a one-room, rural-Wisconsin school house (Allen School) during the early 1940s, my mom knew the circumstances I faced when I entered that same school as a first grader some seven years later.

The teacher had no experience or training in the handling a special-needs child. So, instead of allowing me to flunk first grade, Mom pulled me out of Allen School and taught me first grade at home.

She then finally found an orthopedic school 60 miles away (in Madison) through the Easter Seals Society. I attended Washington Orthopedic School until I completed eighth grade (staying with "house parents" during week and coming home on weekends when Mom would help me with my school assignments and do my laundry).

## Second: High Expectations

My parents and teachers all expected me to do well in school.

In third grade, I remember struggling with my multiplication tables and couldn't remember that three times nine was 27. Miss Van Tassell and Miss McKillip, both blessed with hearty laughter, teamed up to help me never to forget that three times nine was 27.

It became our comic routine. In the hallway, at lunch or in therapy at Washington Orthopedic School, I would suddenly be quizzed by the staff people, "Jim, what are three times nine?" I would proudly answer, "27," and everyone would laugh, including myself.

## Third: Achievement Motivated

Somehow I always felt motivated to do well in school because my parents expected it of me. I had gotten the message: My future depended on getting good grades.

So, even though I would cry on Monday mornings, knowing I would have to leave my family for a whole week and stay in Madison to go to school, I knew it was what I had to do. My crying would stop by Monday noon once I was in the school routine.

By fifth grade, I knew if I continued to do well in school, there was possibility that I could go to my small, rural (but "regular") high school back home. That possibility continued to propel me. But, the thought of attending a "regular" school "in the country" was scary, too.

# Fourth: Caring

As an elementary student who was feeling "displaced" during the week, dealing with the dread that my mom would die (she was being treated for breast cancer at that time) and learning how to cope with CP, I was hardly focused on the needs of others and how I could help other people in need.

Yet, I remember my mom speaking with me in a rather adult conversation one Friday night on the way home from Spring Green, WI, where she picked me up from the Greyhound bus ride out of Madison, WI, where I went to school.

"I have good news," she said excitedly. "Paul (my younger brother by three years) just won a Schwinn bike in a coloring contest. He's so proud."

She wanted me, as a nine-year-old, to make sure I paid special attention to Paul's success and to help him feel good about it. I knew what she meant, even at that age. Having an older brother with a disability who seemed to get much attention from Mom and Dad as well as others was not easy. Here was my chance to show I cared about what he had achieved.

# Fifth: Decision Making

From second grade on, I could see that life included making some tough decisions because I was involved in charting the course I would take.

I remember my mom discussing the option of attending Washington Orthopedic School and what that would all entail for me. I truly feared that transition but realized, even at seven, I had to do it. I had very few alternatives, and the one we chose turned out to be the best.

The transition to a regular high school (small and rural) was mainly my decision. My eighth-grade classmates thought I was rather foolish, since I had the opportunity to attend a high school in Madison, which offered much more in terms of courses and extracurricular activities.

By the time I was in high school, I was comfortable with making decisions.

## Sixth: Personal Power

Because of my early decision making experience, I felt empowered as a youngster. I felt I had some influence over the things that were happening in my life, although I was shy and had not yet learned how to be assertive.

I learned to be assertive because my parents had always provided options for me. I gradually learned to uncover my own options, which I especially needed when I entered the work world.

## Seventh: Sense of Purpose

I remember my mom giving me a reason for making choices and striving to make the best of them: "God has a purpose for you."

It's taken me six decades to figure out what that purpose is (an insight that still may be not as clear as I'd like it to be), but, at eight years old, the promise of a purpose in life was a powerful motivator.

In spite of all the difficulties of growing up with CP, life, in a series of fleeting but memorable moments, became an adventure for me because it turned out to be full of surprises.

Those are seven career development skills I hope you have an opportunity to foster in your youngster over the years as a career-coaching parent.

# STRATEGY 10 – LAY THE FOUNDATION FOR CAREER DEVELOPMENT

Careers are built over a lifetime, and your youngster's career development plan will change many times over the years from elementary school through adulthood.

## Four Stages of Career Development

According to the Oregon Department of Education, the stages of a career development plan are most often associated with age. During the elementary grades, your youngster is likely to be involved in the awareness stage; in middle school, the exploration stage; in high school, college and early adulthood, the planning and preparation stages; and the establishment and transition stages throughout his or her adult life.

Your youngster's career development plan also depends on his or her "career maturity" and circumstances which may be affected by his or her disability.

Career maturity relates to an individual's readiness to perform career-related tasks. To perform tasks, a person needs a positive attitude, skills, and knowledge.

It is important to understand that your youngster will progress through the career development process at his or her own pace. At some point, the stages may even overlap. Or your youngster may go back to an earlier stage. If you can recognize your youngster's stage of career development, you will know how to better provide needed support.

Schools engage students in classroom career activities. Because they are working with a group of students, the activities are generally designed to address a specific developmental stage. This assumes all students are at that same stage, and this most likely is not the case.

So, if your youngster is struggling with an assigned career-related task, consider if he or she has the skills and knowledge to complete the task.

As your youngster moves through school, you will become increasingly involved in his or her career development. After high school, your involvement will likely decrease, but your continued support is just as vital. Even with the best planning, it is not unusual for children to be indecisive about their careers well into their twenties.

And, just as with anything else in life, there are no guarantees. The most carefully shaped career development plan will not prevent mistakes, unforeseen events, or unusual circumstances beyond your control.

However, by helping your youngster acquire career skills and gain self-confidence in "I can do this," you're helping him or her move forward.

## Career Awareness

The lifelong process of career development begins as early as four years old. In these early years, you can begin to instill hope and confidence about the future by helping your youngster discover the world and how he or she will be able to best navigate in it as an independent adult.

This awareness stage involves discovery, imagination, and curiosity. Your youngster is fascinated by everyday things. He or she wants to know more about the things happening in the family, the community and the world.

Your youngster may have a career fantasy that is totally unrealistic. That's OK.

When I was about six, I was convinced that I wanted to be a carpenter, a builder, because I saw most of the men in my life on our farm with a hammer or some sort of tool hanging out of their bibbed overalls, and I thought hammers were so cool. Of course, it was unrealistic. But, I enjoyed imitating my adult world.

At the elementary level, a career development plan usually revolves around career-related activities which often focus on:

- Self-awareness.

- Development of a positive attitude about learning and doing.

- Development of skills to make decisions.

- Knowledge of the broad characteristics and expectations of work.

As a career-coaching parent or mentor, you play a vital role in encouraging your youngster to explore various careers through play and dress up, reading and talking, exploring and learning – even though they're "fantasy careers."
It is never too early to begin talking to your youngster about personal gifts, talents and interests. Your youngster will do better in school and begin to recognize that disability can have a competitive advantage, if he or she believes personal success is obtainable.

# STRATEGY 11 – TEACH TEAMWORK SKILLS

Teamwork building for the elementary student with special needs you're mentoring sometimes gets down to turning around the idea that individuals with disabilities are takers and not givers.

I still remember the anguish I'd feel each morning when I was about six. I knew I would have to tie my own shoes. I had no option.

Of course, Mom could have easily tied my shoes for me. I could have learned to always be a taker – to always receive help, even though I knew I could help myself.

Turning that thinking around – that I was entitled to always receive help instead of sometimes giving it to others – came as a result, I believe, of my home environment, where teamwork building was a skill developed as a result of doing chores.

Growing up on a Wisconsin dairy farm in the 1950s meant everyone in the family pitched in to get the barn and household chores done during the winter months. During summertime, there were pies to bake for the extra field hands and gathering, gardening and canning to do.

Gardening was my task, and I remember sitting and crawling between the rows of peas, pulling weeds.

Somehow, the teamwork building I saw on a daily basis before I entered school as a second grader (my mom taught me first grade at home) stuck with me as I grew up. I knew I had an obligation to others.

So, I'm sometimes puzzled about why we assume the "abled" give and disabled people take. Like the other dualities of our time and cultures, we think people are good or bad, friends or enemies, abled or disabled, and givers or takers.

But, in fact, giving and taking is a circle where no one is above or below, first or last, further along or further behind. That's the foundation of teamwork building.

## Teamwork-building Exercise

Here's a career-centered exercise you can do with your youngster for demonstrating teamwork building skills. Have your youngster interview you about your own school and career experiences when you were young.

Your youngster might ask:

- What were your favorite school subjects?

- What did you like to do with your free time?

- What career did you think about when you were young?

- Did you follow your dreams? Why or why not?

- What did your parents want you to do?

- Who helped you make your education and career decisions?

- What did you learn in school that helped you the most?

- What is your favorite thing about the work you do now?

- What do you like least about the work you do now?

- What did you learn in elementary school that you use in your work now?

- What did you learn in elementary school that you use in your home life?

Such an interview (or conversation) – no matter how informal it is – places your youngster into a "giving" mode because an interviewer automatically becomes a facilitator.

Your youngster is tapping your knowledge and experience – for the benefit of both of you.

# STRATEGY 12 – SHOW
# HOW TO SET AND ACHIEVE GOALS

I remember passing notes between my mom and my third grade teach on a regular basis. Just that pre-cell phone, pre-Internet means of communication in 1953 told me that both were working for my welfare and I'd better "toe the line" (whatever that meant in terms of homework, behaving in class, not being so weepy etc.).

That's how I believe goal setting for kids starts. Your youngster recognizes your dedication to his or her well-being simply by observing your day-to-day activities which are the result of the goal setting you've done, either in your head or on the keyboard.

Goal setting for kids is practicing that skill and setting an example as a career-coaching parent of your elementary student with special needs so he or she can become familiar with the process.

## High Expectations and Praise

I noticed those notes each Monday and Friday in 1953 as I made the trek between our home farm and my orthopedic school often yielded some form of praise from my mom or from my teacher.

As you engage in goal setting for youngster, find reasons to praise your youngster every day. By doing so, you're reinforcing his or her talents and strengths. That shows your youngster that you believe he or she is a valuable and capable individual who will live a meaningful life as an adult.

As a "guest" in the homes of the four "house parents' I had between second and eighth grade, I knew what mom expected: that I behave and be polite during the week in my dealings with the mom and dad of the family and their kids in my Madison "home."

It was my responsibility because I was basically functioning without her supervision for five days out of every week. So, I automatically knew what goal setting for kids was all about by the time I was eight.

Goal setting for kids involves having high expectations for learning and behavior, both at home and at school. When you expect the best from your youngster, he or she will rise to your expectations.

## Examples of Goal Setting for Kids

Make sure your youngster is getting the best education possible by working directly with your school and its teachers. How do you do that?

Here are some goal-setting tips for kids from state of Oregon's Partnership for Occupational and Career Information:

### Talk with your youngster's teachers.

- Arrange a time to observe the teaching in your youngster's classroom, if possible.

### Talk with your youngster about his or her schoolwork.

- Discuss how the skills your youngster is learning in school are an important part of everyday life.

### Help your youngster develop routines.

- Have regular homework or reading time.

### Teach your youngster to love to read.

- Read to your youngster from an early age.

### Create a study environment in your home.

- Do not allow the TV to be on while your youngster is doing homework.

- Make a "study area" that has paper, pencils, pens, erasers, a dictionary and other materials your youngster uses to do schoolwork.

**Spend time with your youngster at home.**

- Use car time to talk with, and listen to, your children.

- Take walks or ride bikes together.

- Eat dinner together, using the time to talk about the day's events.

Goal setting for kids doesn't have to be difficult or complicated. It's a matter of showing your youngster how it works in everyday life. Each of the suggestions above can be one of your goals for career coaching your elementary school youngster with special needs.

# STRATEGY 13 – TAKE SMALL STEPS TO ACHIEVE A GOAL

Here's a message for your elementary school youngster with special needs:

> You can realize your dreams if you dream big (like George Bailey in "It's a Wonderful Life"), create a vision for yourself, show your passion, develop patience and connect with people who can influence your future.

That's what Dr. Samantha Collins, CEO of Aspire Companies and founder of The Aspire Foundation (a mentorship program for women across 24 countries), recommends. She's a recognized leadership expert and executive coach.

One of the Top 100 Coaches in the UK, Collins says identifying your big goal is important because your dreams are your fuel. They motivate you.

She's not a big fan of SMART goals (those which are "specific, measurable, achievable, relevant and time-framed"). She recommends, instead, "developing more of a vision, going to your highest level."

She adds, "You don't have to be realistic at this stage. Your vision should invoke excitement as well as slight terror -- terror because you're clueless about how you're going to pull it all off. All the planning can come later."

That may be just the right touch for your youngster with special needs, who is now ready to learn about steps to setting a goal.

## Develop a Dream Board

Collins reminds us that, in order to achieve, your youngster needs to fail and learn how to get up and try again. Learning how to live with failure develops persistence, agility and resiliency -- all key attributes employers seek in job candidates.

Your youngster develops that persistence, agility and resiliency by learning how to bounce back quickly in the face of adversity (in minutes -- or in a day at the maximum), Collins points out. "Go to the next level of deciding what to do differently next time and then practice so you really do it differently," she recommends.

In other words, being authentic and knowing what you need to know to do better next time will draw people to you who can help your realize your dream. That advice about steps to setting a goal applies to not only your youngster but to you, as a "career coach."

Thinking "I'm lucky" or "I'm a super person" are both pitfalls because when some things don't work out like you had hoped (and that will most likely happen along the way as you career coach your youngster), you can easily start thinking, "I'm a fraud," Collins points out. In other words, true personal power is being comfortable with yourself and your capabilities -- being authentic.

Develop a 'dream board' for pulling your youngster into the future, she recommends. You can do that together by following these steps to making a dream that may seem fuzzy more concrete and obtainable:

- **Create** a collage of magazine pictures, newspaper headlines etc. which resonate with your youngster because they illustrate, in concrete terms, what his or her dream is all about.

- **Make** sure your youngster puts him or herself in the center of that dream board.

- **Place** it in a location where you both can see it frequently on a daily basis.

- **Take** one small, achievable action toward your youngster's dream within 24 hours of creating the dream board so you both feel like you're already a part of it.

- **Work** together toward making your youngster's dream board come true, one step at a time, perhaps with the help of his or her teacher.

- **Go** onto a new dream board when your youngster has accomplished what was first envisioned.

By following that process, Collins asserts, you'll both get to know yourselves better and learn that preparing for an eventual career is a long process of small steps toward achieving an overarching goal.

Discovering Disability's Competitive Advantage

# STRATEGY 14 – DEVELOP
# PROBLEM-SOLVING ABILITY

Here are some problem solving activities designed to help your elementary student with special needs acquire skills in communication and teamwork, two key attributes which will continue to be essential in tomorrow's workplace.

## Improving Communication Skills

Communication includes reading, writing, listening, and speaking. Keep lots of quality reading material around the house. Make visits to the library part of your family routine. Point out that pleasurable reading comes from good writing.

Here are some ideas for helping your youngster develop better communication skills:

- **Read** to your youngster, and have your youngster read to you. Let your youngster see you read at least 20 minutes a day.

- **Encourage** good listening. Discuss the content of what you or your youngster has read. Tell stories, and have your youngster re-tell them in detail.

- **Play** games that involve writing, speaking, listening and imagination. Charades requires non-verbal skills.

- **Encourage** writing. Expect that your youngster will write letters and thank you notes to relatives and friends. Make sure your youngster has writing materials, such as journals and diaries, available.

## Improving Teamwork

Teams are not only important on the athletic field. All aspects of life require people to work effectively as members of teams. Think of your family as a team, and use some of these ideas:

- **Build your family team.** Involve your youngster in family discussions or decisions, as appropriate for his or her age and maturity level.

- **Work together.** Give your youngster important jobs to do within the family or work on chores together.

- **Practice conflict resolution.** Teach your youngster to get along with others by modeling good teamwork and conflict resolution.

- **Learn together.** Emphasize the learning that takes place in groups, whether on school projects or team activities like sports, music, theater, or volunteering.

## Laying an Employment Foundation

Employment requires understanding and using tools and technology, working in organizations and systems, and following procedures. You can help your youngster begin building these skills at home by:

- **Doing projects** that require many steps, use of tools, and following procedures, such as:

    ✓ Cooking together (your youngster could read recipes and measure ingredients).

✓ Doing laundry (your youngster could sort items of clothing according to color, read washing instructions, measure detergent and time wash cycles).

✓ Going grocery shopping (have your youngster write shopping lists, compare food prices, make change, and identify and classify food items).

✓ Fixing the family photo album (have your youngster sort pictures, write labels for each photo or write a story about some of the photos).

✓ Organizing the house (have your youngster sort items in a "junk drawer," label them and arrange them alphabetically).

- **Talking** about products and services you use. Introduce your youngster to all aspects of work, including technology, business, artistic, social and customer service perspectives.

- **Discussing** new technologies and how they change our lives. Discuss ways to improve products, processes and services with your youngster. Encourage him or her to brainstorm solutions to technical and human problems.

You are your youngster's first teacher when it comes to learning how to solve problems.

# STRATEGY 15 – RIDE ONLY ONE HORSE

Today, those ready for the job market can choose the managerial/executive route or the hands-on route within a large corporate environment or choose to do a little bit of both within a small company.

They can gain experience by making a series of lateral moves within one organization to better prepare ourselves for targeted positions, or they can reach that same type of position by gaining the required experience through vertical moves by working for several different companies within a specific job sector. Or they can hone their skill sets in a variety of jobs in a variety of industries.

In short, there are a lot of horses to ride – not just one. And, that puts a premium on career choice information. Look ahead 10 to 15 years from now, and, you can expect career choices to be even more diversified than they are today once your youngster begins to search for a job.

That's why I believe it's important for you, as a "career coaching" parent or mentor, to stay tuned into the current career choice information provided by the U.S. Department of Labor.

On today's workplace racing track, those who have chosen the right horse for themselves (and stuck with it) are more likely to find fulfillment in their careers. I think that one factor may remain constant during the coming years.

My one bit of advice in terms of career choice for your elementary student with special needs is this: Ride only one horse.

That may seem like a premature mentoring tip. And, it may not even seem wise because, even today, the career paths and job sectors open to your youngster are becoming increasingly diverse.

But, ride one horse. That bit of career choice information could become crucial in your youngster's career development. Let me explain why.

## Choose to Ride Only One Horse

Within an environment of multiple options, your youngster can easily get mired in career choice  and lose sight of the need to first focus on his or her unique temperament, behavior and ability. They are the essential considerations in managing one's career.

Let me introduce to Susan. At the beginning of college, she was excited about becoming a dentist. That fascination with dentistry lasted about nine months. She then picked up an interest in industrial psychiatry but dropped out of college in her senior year to work for an Internet startup in customer service. At 25, she's now is toying with the idea of becoming firefighter. But she really doesn't have concrete plans about how to do that either.

Dentistry, industrial psychiatry, firefighting. Is there one horse? Is there a common skill set in those occupations?

Susan reminds me of Harley Swiggum. He grew up in rural Wisconsin and served in the Navy during World War II. But, in a series of failed attempts at starting his career within several different job sectors after the war, he became discouraged and confused about how to use the variety of hidden talents he possessed. In a downward spiral, he began to drink and eventually found himself on Skid Row.

The fact is that he had too many ways to tap his talents, and he lacked the career choice information we have today online that could have helped him in his career decision making.

He's now Dr. Harley Swiggum, founder the Adult Christian Education Foundation and The Bethel Series. Here's his advice, based on personal experience: Find the horse that's right for you, and then ride it and ride to the hilt.

Let me extrapolate in career coaching terms what I believe Dr. Swiggum is saying:

To successfully build a career, you need to identify the horse that's right for you -- a personal mission that will grow into a framework which will eventually help you make career decisions that are right for you. That's not easy because it means you need to first know yourself, identify what you value and create a vision for yourself. You'll discover your personal mission (horse) over time as your self-knowledge, values and vision take on a sharper focus.

A personal mission is a short, concise statement of what your youngster is fitted to do in life. As your youngster matures, he or she can begin to form a personal mission statement by answering these three questions:

- What do I do that is unique to me?

- Whom do I serve?

- How do the people I serve benefit?

This means the most helpful career choice information is often inside us. As we mature, we are able to tap into that "internal GPS" that is in all of us.

As career-coaching parent or mentor, you can help your youngster lay the foundation for such an approach to career management by providing him or her with career choice information (an awareness of the possibilities and what's ahead) now.

And a healthy career outlook, based on that career choice information, can mean your youngster will be a length ahead of his or her competitors whenever he or she makes an important career move.

# STRATEGY 16 – EXPLORE
# THE WORLD OF WORK

The lifelong process of career development begins as early as four years old and extends into what we once called "retirement."

In these early years, you, as a career-coaching parent, can begin to instill hope and confidence about the future by helping your youngster discover him or herself as well as the world of work.

The awareness stage involves discovery, imagination, and curiosity. Young children are fascinated by everyday things. They want to know more about things they observe in their families, their communities, and the world.

Many of their interests are displayed in career fantasies. They enjoy imitating the adult world. You play a vital role in encouraging your children through play and dress up, reading and talking, exploring and learning.

At seven, my career fantasy was to become a carpenter. I wanted to build things – to create. Today, at 71, I'm still a builder, despite my CP. I've had a career of almost 50 years of building. I just didn't use brick and mortar and a hammer. I used a keyboard.

In grade school, career-related learning expands awareness of oneself and the world of work. It helps connect school to real life. You might remember a visit to the neighborhood fire station from your own elementary years.

Most elementary teachers now imbed career awareness into their curriculum on a regular basis. Their academic goals often include learning about the community and roles in society. Real life examples, through classroom trips, presentations, or projects, are the learning foundation for today's career information for kids.

You can support career-related learning at your youngster's elementary school by:

- **Finding** out about the career-related learning goals and program at the school.

- **Talking** about the career events and activities with your youngster.

- **Helping** your youngster reflect on what he or she learned from these events and activities ("What did you find interesting?" "What did not interest you?" "What does that tell you about yourself?").

- **Participating** in career events and activities as a volunteer.

- **Talking** to your employer and other acquaintances about volunteering when the school needs the larger community to join you in working together on a community project.

Career information for kids in the early years is building the foundation for the upper grades. These activities are not meant in any way to track your youngster onto a particular path. Instead, they are important in setting the stage by stimulating curiosity, making connections, and building a sense of community.

Understanding the world of work is important for preparing for all of these life roles. It is the first step your youngster takes in eventually formulating a career plan.

In fact understanding the world of work follows closely with the various stages of your youngster's career development.

First, your youngster needs to be aware that career development is a lifelong process. Later, he or she will explore, through investigation and experience, personal interests, values, and skills.

As a participant in the world of work, your son or daughter will need to continue to keep informed about personal career development so he or she can effectively and actively manage his or her career.

It's never too early for your youngster to begin observing the adult world and its number of interrelated life roles: learner, producer, consumer, family member, and citizen. As a parent, you are acting as a role-model for your youngster in each case.

# STRATEGY 17 – REACH
# FOR THREE DEVELOPMENTAL MILESTONES

I've identified three developmental milestones (learning, dependability and acceptance) after listening for two decades to what employees with special needs say have made them successful and to what employers say they seek in job applicants.

More precisely, those three developmental milestones are an orientation toward lifelong learning (learning), persistence in working toward a goal (dependability) and an appreciation for differences in people (acceptance).

Of course, the attributes employers seek today in applicants they interview for open jobs are different than they were in 1980 and 1990 because the whole work environment has changed and technology has changed. But, the basic needs of employers still remain. They need new employees who know how to learn, are persistent in pursuing a goal and value differences in people.

Imagine your youngster as a job seeker 20 years from now. Will he or she have reached the required developmental milestones so they can match what employers currently seek in a job candidate?

Will those attributes still be relevant two decades from now? I think so. Here is how I define each of these attributes:

## Learning

- **You** are keeping your skills fresh through continuing education and training.

- **You're** dedicated to lifelong learning; you don't have all the answers but are willing to (and know how to) find them.

- **You're** open to change, you continually challenge yourself to improve your skills and you are flexible so you can be cross-trained laterally as well as vertically; you'll be able to learn the job to the side of you as well as in front of you.

- **You're** an innovator and problem solver and are willing to take a reasonable risk.

- **You** know information technology.

As a person with a special needs, your youngster is going to have a real opportunity to demonstrate his or her ability to learn and to commit to lifelong learning.

If your youngster uses any type of assistive technology (AT) at all, for instance, he or she will have an opportunity to show future employers how keeping up with advances in AT on a yearly basis is work-related experience other job applicants without a disability may not have had. That's an employment edge your youngster will be able to promote as a job seeker, if you both prepare for it now, together.

Becoming an assistive technology expert – someone who can help an employer easily and economically install any on-the-job accommodations your youngster may need to carry out his or her duties within the workforce of 2030 – is, I believe, one of the key developmental milestones you both can begin to tackle at the elementary school level.

## Motivation

- **You** can demonstrate your work ethic so your supervisor knows he or she can depend on you.

- **You're** dedicated to doing a good job.

- **You'll** take the initiative.

- **You'll** go the extra mile.

- **You** truly want the job at hand.

- **You** have crystallized your life story and can present it effectively in terms of how it shows you can meet employer needs.

Dependability is the key here. Your elementary school youngster can begin writing personal experience stories (perhaps in an online diary) which show he or she has learned how to live well with a disability through persistence (the foundation of dependability).

Then, your youngster will someday be in a position to show how he or she has learned to transfer that persistence to the workplace – an attribute that will increase the resiliency of an employer's workforce precisely because your youngster has learned how to be persistent and reliable in working toward a goal.

So, one of the key developmental milestones for your elementary school youngster is developing the reputation for being reliable.

## Teamwork

- **You** are a team player.

- **You** can be a bridge between generations within your work group, showing others how to approach work in ways they have not yet encountered.

- **You** can work effectively with a variety of people.

- **You're** a good communicator.

- **You're** well-rounded -- you don't have a 4.0 grade average, and that's OK because you have participated in a variety of activities while gaining your education.

- **You** can handle stress.

As an individual with special needs, your youngster will likely find his or herself, at times, with one foot in the non-disabled and the other in disabled world -- and trying to effectively relate to both at the same time. That can be valuable experience.

Over the years, look for opportunities to show your youngster that he or she can be a bridge builder and be an example to others about how to value differences in people. Isn't that one of the most important developmental milestones for your youngster?

Think of the differences in generations we have today. Baby boomers approach work from a different perspective than those who are in the generation X category, for example. Employers sometimes have up to four generations represented in their workforces, and they need experienced bridge builders. They need individuals who value (and celebrate) differences in people.

That situation may or may not change in the next 20 years. But, the traditional concept of retirement is fast fading, and the U.S. is becoming a nation of minorities -- no longer best described as white, male and Protestant.

In fact, developing an orientation toward learning, dependability and acceptance at an early age will give your youngster the foundation for meeting the needs future employers will seek in job candidates two decades from now.

The good news is that learning how to live well with a disability will help develop those attributes in your youngster. You can use disability to help frame what learning, dependability and acceptance mean in preparation for future challenges your youngster will face in finding meaningful work.

# SUMMARY

Help your elementary school youngster grow in self-confidence. Here are nine strategies for accomplishing that goal:

**Strategy 1: Learn What It Means to Work** – Talk to your youngster about occupational interests and the specific jobs and job titles which are associated with those interests.

**Strategy 2: Nurture Self-esteem** – Help your youngster grow in self-esteem.

**Strategy 3: Address Fear** – Provide opportunities for your youngster to express his or her feelings of insecurity – through drawing, diaries, play acting, casual chats etc. as a part of "growing up."

**Strategy 4: Manage Motivation** - Provide a range of experiences through sports, music, volunteer activities, and travel so your youngster can discover and develop his or her strengths, bolster self-confidence and acquire the motivation to do more.

**Strategy 5: Value Patience** - Learned patience (particularly patience developed within a good skill set through personal struggle to reach a long-term goal at an early age) may be just the right attribute for tomorrow's jobs -- jobs your elementary student with special needs of today could perhaps someday hold.

**Strategy 6: Use Visual Learning** – Use the "handy tips" exercise to help your youngster grow in self-confidence by identifying in concrete terms what they're "good at doing."

**Strategy 7: Learn Virtual Team-building Skills -** Tap current virtual learning opportunities now while your youngster with special needs is still in elementary school to give him or her a "leg up" in tomorrow's job market.

**Strategy 8: Start Career Planning Now** - Between the ages of four and 10, your son or daughter will likely form a lasting impression of what life is all about and how he she can fit into it. Make sure the basics of career planning are a part of that initial impression.

**Strategy 9: Foster Seven Career Development Skills** – These are common-sense, positive experiences and qualities that help influence choices young people make and help them become caring, responsible, successful adults.

Help your elementary school youngster discover disability's competitive advantage Here are eight strategies for accomplishing that goal:

**Strategy 10: Lay the Foundation for Career Development** - During the elementary grades, your youngster is likely to be involved in the awareness stage.

**Strategy 11: Teach Teamwork Skills -** Teamwork building for the elementary student with special needs you're mentoring sometimes gets down to turning around the idea that individuals with disabilities are takers and not givers.

**Strategy 12: Show How to Set and Achieve Goals** - Goal setting for kids is practicing that skill and setting an example as a career-coaching parent.

**Strategy 13: Take Small Steps to Achieve a Goal -** Develop a 'dream board' for pulling your youngster into the future. You can do that together by setting a goal of making a dream that may seem fuzzy more concrete and obtainable.

**Strategy 14: Develop Problem-solving Ability** – Collect problem solving activities designed to help your elementary student with special needs acquire skills in communication and teamwork, two key attributes which will continue to be essential in tomorrow's workplace.

**Strategy 15: Ride Only One Horse** - You can expect career choices to be even more diversified than they are today once your youngster begins to search for a job. Stay tuned into the current career choice information provided by the U.S. Department of Labor and encourage your youngster to focus on one promising job sector.

**Strategy 16: Explore the World of Work -** Begin to instill hope and confidence about the future by helping your youngster discover him or herself as well as the world of work.

**Strategy 17: Reach for Three Developmental Milestones** - Three key developmental milestones are an orientation toward lifelong learning (learning), persistence in working toward a goal (dependability) and an appreciation for differences in people (acceptance). Cultivate those three attributes in your youngster now.

I wish you much success in carrying out these 17 key career-building strategies for your elementary school youngster.

# NATIONAL CAREER DEVELOPMENT GUIDELINES

According to the National Career Development Guidelines (NCDG), here are 10 important career skills your youngster can develop during elementary school:

- **Identify** personal interests, likes, and dislikes.

- **Describe** personal strengths and talents.

- **Demonstrate** positive behaviors and personal characteristics, such as honesty, dependability, responsibility, integrity, and loyalty.

- **Recognize** that one should accept responsibility for one's behavior.

- **Interact** with others in a fair, helpful, and respectful way.

- **Recognize** that people have many life roles and that these need to be balanced.

- **Demonstrate** study skills and good learning habits.

- **Be** able to set goals and work toward achieving them.

- **Describe** different ways to make decisions.
- **Recognize** a variety of skills (such as communicating, critical thinking, problem solving, and interpersonal skills) that are important for success in school and work.

# LAST THOUGHTS

If I had to select one word which describes what it's like to grow up with a lifelong disability such as CP, it would be "fear."

However, I remember my dad saying he was shy as a kid but that he gradually grew out of it. So, I'm not sure if my insecurity is in my gene pool, in how I was raised or in how I personally reacted to my CP.

For years, I held my fear inside, and, when I was about 10 years old, I truly felt I was psychologically unstable because I didn't how to manage fear and I never discussed it openly with my parents.

I told no one that I feared I was psychologically unstable because I was afraid a good deal of the time when I was outside my "safe" environment (i.e. home). My insecurity was producing a fear that something was "wrong" with me.

As a five-year-old, I feared being left by my parents with others -- even with a familiar baby sitter. And, I remember the panic I felt one evening when I was left in a church pew alone because my parents temporarily stepped out of the sanctuary.

In grade school, I feared walking down the aisle of any public forum (movie theatre, church, school etc.) because I would picture myself falling in front of the crowd due to my stiff legs and the pitiful stares I would get from onlookers because of my CP.

In high school, I clung to the hallway lockers for fear I would be trampled by the bigger, more "normal" students, especially the guys in black leather jackets and ducktails (yes, it was the 1950s). I also had an aversion to three-foot wastebaskets because one time a fellow student (a hefty Wisconsin farm girl) had to fish me out of one. I had grabbed it for balance and, instead, flew head first (and arms) into the trash.

The summer before my first year in college, I silently cried in the back seat during a family car trip out West when my mom reminded me that my first college classes started in just three weeks. I knew I wasn't ready to face that new environment, and I dreaded even thinking about it during a carefree (and safe) summer vacation.

During college, I settled into a comfortable routine but worried about how I would fare after graduation when I would enter the rough and tumble "real world." Real-world business people, I thought, would hear my slurred speech and immediately discount my intelligence and training. And, I wouldn't be able to get a job.

But, for me, failure, at that point, was not an option. In my experience, there was no advantage to failure. By growing up on a farm, I knew what a crop failure meant: less feed, less milk, less income, less freedom.

As a young person with CP, I needed to earn an income to become independent -- to be the first in our family to get a non-farm job. Yet, once on the job, I feared being suffocated in unchallenging work within a "going nowhere" company in a back-water rural area.

But, by the time I became 30 years old, I began to realize some success (and recognition by others) in my work as a corporate communicator, and that helped me learn how to manage my anxiety.

I found that people generally don't think much about what makes others "different" because they are often preoccupied with their own concerns. And, I learned that organizations, especially my employer, tend to change through one "pocket" at a time instead of top down (at the leadership of the CEO, for instance).

Now that I look back on my career, my "false" fears of failure may have actually crippled my growth. Yet, on the other hand, I'm probably stronger now because I experienced that struggle.

The workarounds for fear that I have developed for myself over the years have made me an innovator and a delegator.

As an innovator, I noticed that people within my workplace were often intrigued by my creativity, even though my ideas may have turned out to be half-baked and not workable at all. At least, they saw that I was thinking -- and thinking in terms of the company's success. Once the company's bottom line became the focus, my CP (and my timidity) seemed to disappear. And, I became more self-confident.

For instance, I worked for a dairy processing cooperative which manufactured commodity cheese in bulk for major food companies. As an upstart during the early 1980s, I found myself asking why, as a highly regarded cheese manufacturer, we should not tap into the value-added portion of the cheese business by developing our own brand and marketing channels so our dairy farmer members could reap increased returns from the milk they produced.

And, as a member of senior management during the 1990s, I was plugging away at the same "value-added" orientation -- only this time as the point person for the organization's strategic planning process.

We were still in the commodity cheese business, but we had developed a whole new value-added product offering: whey products for pharmaceuticals, bakeries, infant formula etc.

In short, I found my CP didn't much matter, if I shifted the focus to innovation. Creativity trumped my CP and deflected any concerns my colleagues may have had about it. And, that made it easier for me.

As I assumed more responsibility and moved into senior management, I also learned how to delegate hands-on work -- especially work that was difficult for me because of my disability.

I started hiring high school students for after-school jobs and then began to offer paid internships for college students. As the organization and my responsibilities grew, I eventually developed a team of five people, each of whom had authority to carry out specific duties (and get the recognition for it).

Over a 28-year span, I hired, trained and developed more than 25 people in the field of corporate communication, public relations and member relations. And, I learned to welcome failure in myself and others because it helped our team grow.

My lack of knowledge about how to manage fear -- my anxiety about what could happen (and often doesn't) because of my CP -- has gradually                                         disappeared.

## ABOUT JIM HASSE, THE AUTHOR

Jim is the founder of <u>cerebral-palsy-career-builders.com</u>, the comprehensive career coaching guide for parents of CP youngsters 7 to 27 years old.

He owns Hasse Communication Counseling, LLC, which helps champions of disability employment form partnerships for win-win direct mail fundraisers.

As a Global Career Developmental Facilitator (GCDF) since 2005, he's the author of 12 Amazon eBooks, each of which explains his central premise: that disability, when framed correctly, can be a competitive advantage in today's job market for job seekers with special needs.

To access his books in electronic as well as soft-cover formats, see http://tinyurl.com/JRH-All-Books-Amazon.

Hasse developed an award-winning corporate communication function for Foremost Farms USA, Baraboo, WI, during his service of 29 years at the cooperative -- 10 of which were at the vice presidential level.

Between 1999 and 2009, he was responsible for all the online content of eSight Careers Network, New York City. As eSight's senior content developer, he wrote, assigned and edited more than 1,300 articles about disability employment issues.

Between 1997 and 2001 (before blogging became commonplace), Hasse developed, facilitated and marketed tell-us-your-story.com, a now-discontinued web site where people with disabilities shared their personal-experience stories and which provided a launching pad for eSight Careers Network.

A 1965 honors graduate of the University of Wisconsin-Madison's School of Journalism, Hasse is an Accredited Business Communicator (ABC) by the International Association of Business Communicators, San Francisco, Calif.

In 1994, he received the Cooperative Spirit Award from the Cooperative Communicators Association (CCA), a national organization for professional communications employed by cooperatives, and the Cooperative Builder Award from a state-wide association of cooperatives in Wisconsin.

In 1995, he received CCA's H.E. Klinefelter Award for distinguished service in cooperative communications.

In addition to his eBooks and soft-cover books, Hasse is the author of "Break Out: Finding Freedom When You Don't Quite Fit The Mold" (Quixote Press, 1996). a memoir of 51 short stories about disability awareness.

He also compiled and edited "Perfectly Able: How to Attract and Hire Talented People with Disabilities" (AMACOM, 2011), a disability recruitment guidebook for hiring managers that highlights disability's competitive advantage in today's job market.

# JIM BOOKS

# 7 TRANSFORMATION STORIES

**Quick Career-insight Series of Seven Little Books**
*for* **Parents of Youngsters with CP**

Each of the seven Little Books takes about 40 minutes to read. Each illustrates and summarizes the essential career builders for your youngster's age group – all through seven transformational stories about Jim Hasse's personal experience as a person with CP.

You'll find considerably more detail about each career builder at <u>cerebral-palsy-career-builders.com</u>, which can be used as an ongoing reference for "how to" information as your youngster matures.

# 7 TRANSFORMATION STORIES

Little Book 1 (Career-coaching Series) about Self-confidence
FOR PARENTS OF ELEMENTARY STUDENTS
with Cerebral Palsy

JIM HASSE

Buy **Little Book 1** on Amazon
at- http://www.amazon.com/dp/B00DPLHRTI

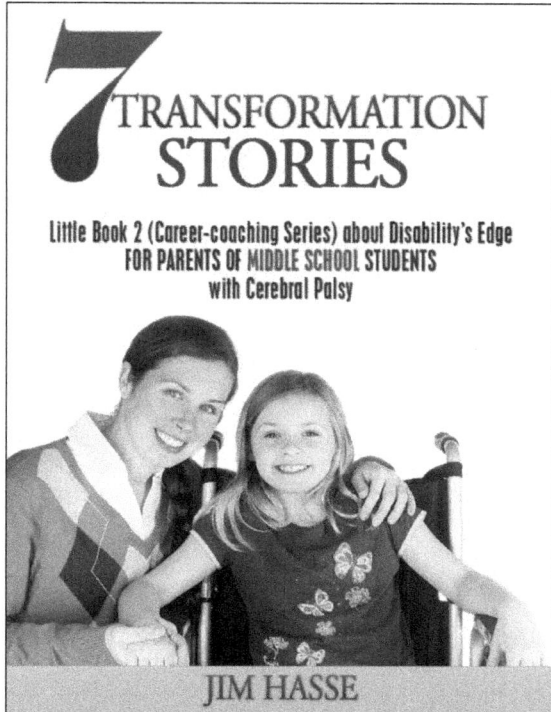

7 TRANSFORMATION STORIES

Little Book 2 (Career-coaching Series) about Disability's Edge
FOR PARENTS OF MIDDLE SCHOOL STUDENTS
with Cerebral Palsy

JIM HASSE

Buy **Little Book 2** on Amazon
at http://www.amazon.com/dp/B00H9WAKHA

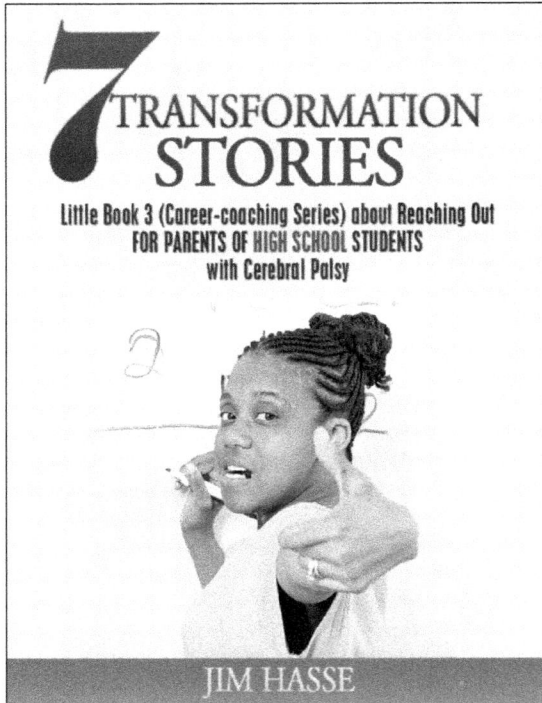

Buy **Little Book 3** on Amazon
at http://www.amazon.com/dp/B00HB77RAQ

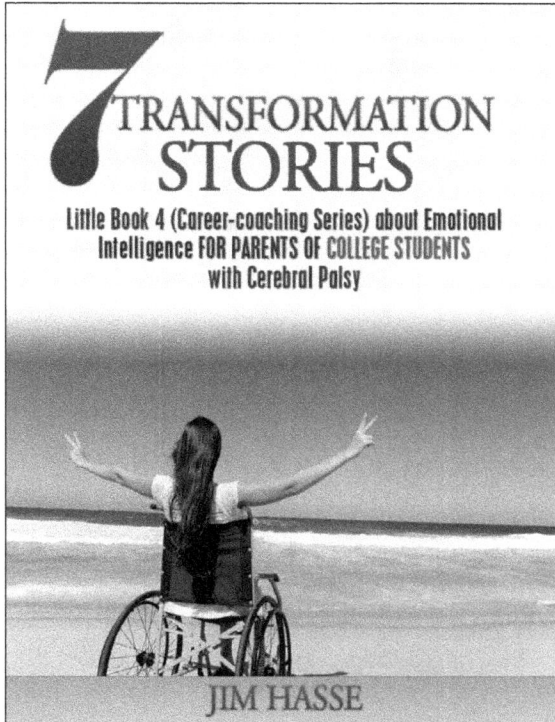

Buy **Little Book 4** on Amazon
at http://www.amazon.com/dp/B00HBDUJ96

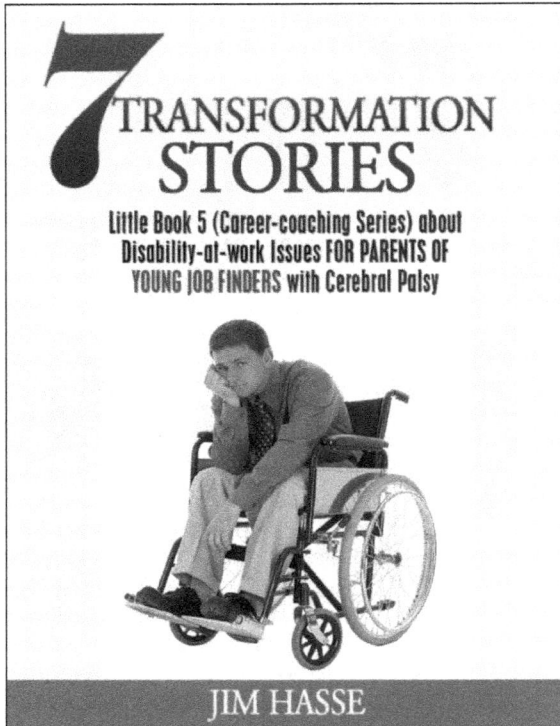

Buy **Little Book 5** on Amazon
at http://www.amazon.com/dp/B00HBVTZ02

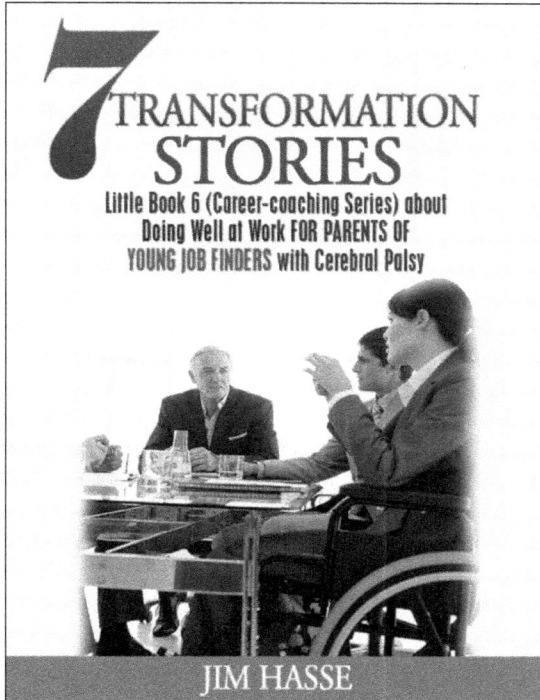

Buy **Little Book 6** on Amazon
at http://www.amazon.com/dp/B00HE60J8G

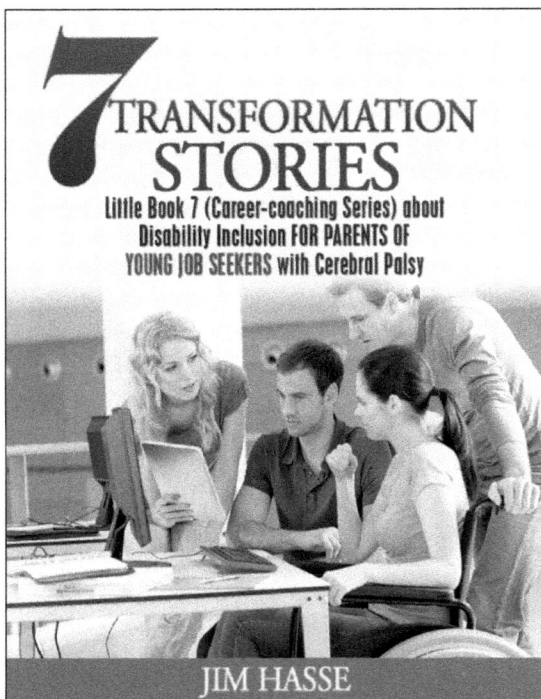

Buy **Little Book 7** on Amazon
at http://www.amazon.com/dp/B00HEVJYUU

**Five Books *for* Parenting Youngsters with Special Needs**

# CAREER BOOK

Each of these five books (available in electronic and paperback formats) takes about 40 minutes to read. Each illustrates and summarizes the essential career development strategies to follow for your youngster's age group – all based on the roadmap recommended by National Career Development Guidelines (NCDG) and Jim Hasse's experience as a Global Career Development Facilitator and as a person with cerebral palsy and mainstream work experience.

You'll find considerably more detail about each career building strategy at www.cerebral-palsy-career-builders.com, which can be used as an ongoing reference for "how to" information as your youngster matures.

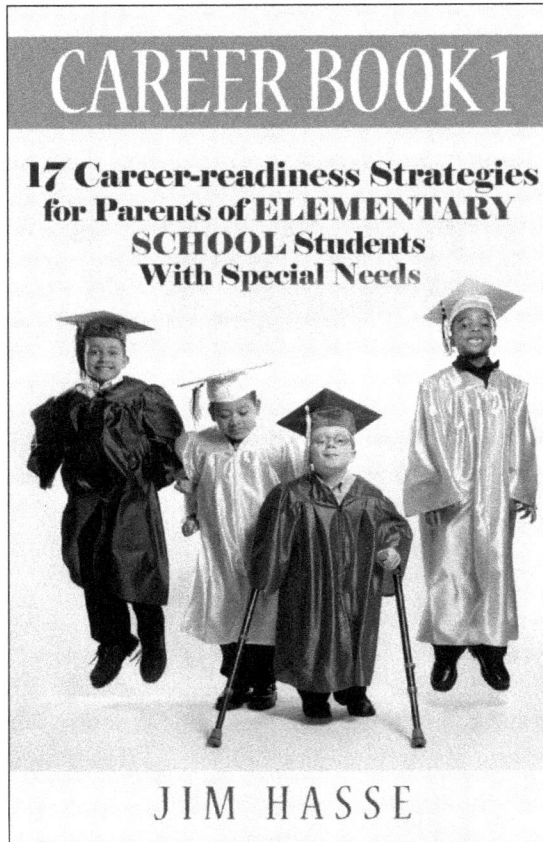

Buy **Career Book 1** on Amazon
at http://www.amazon.com/dp/B00JNYH6JM

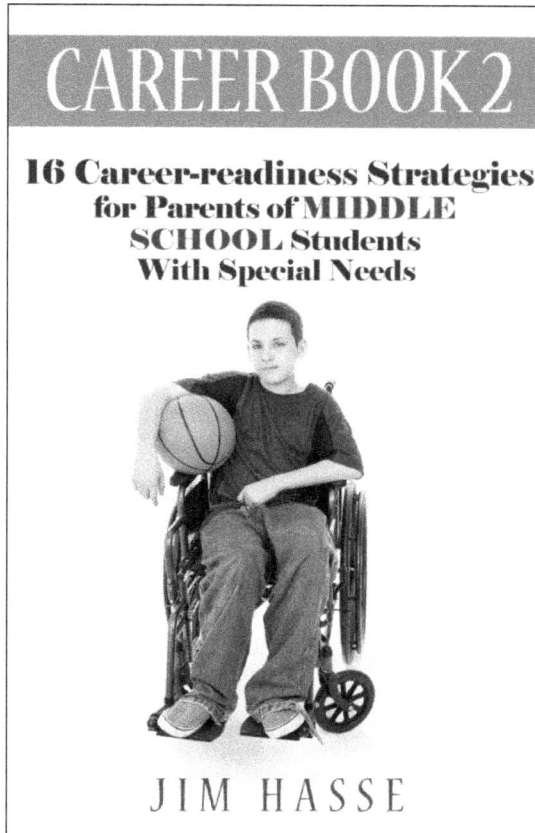

Buy **Career Book 2** on Amazon
at http://www.amazon.com/dp/B00KLIMPBS

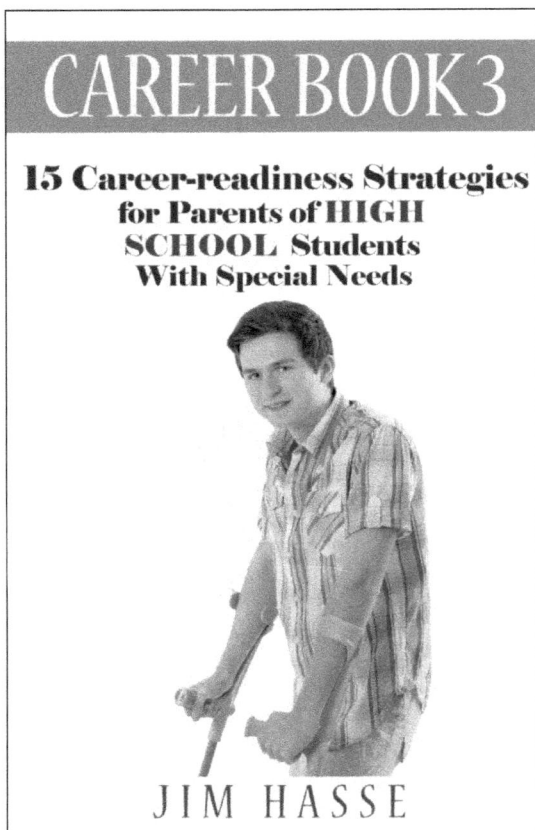

Buy **Career Book 3** on Amazon
at http://www.amazon.com/dp/B00KN2OF56

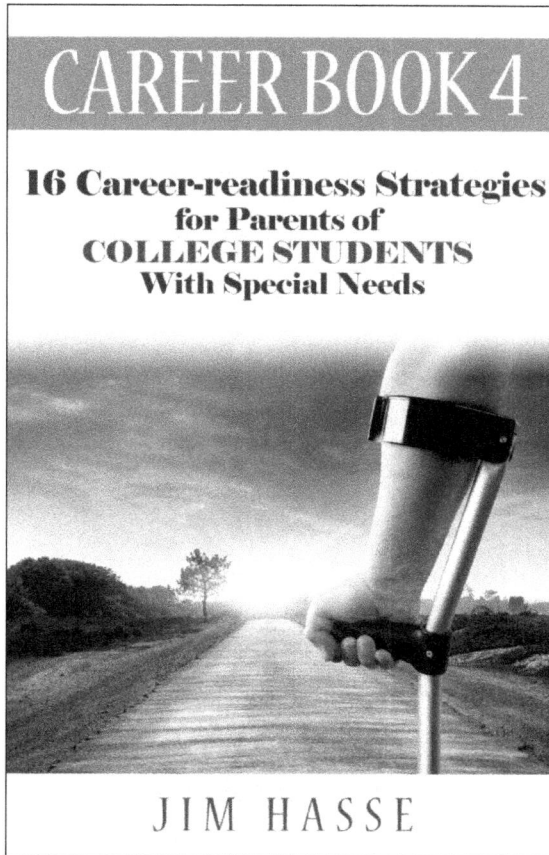

Buy **Career Book 4** on Amazon
at http://www.amazon.com/dp/B00KPGV5B2

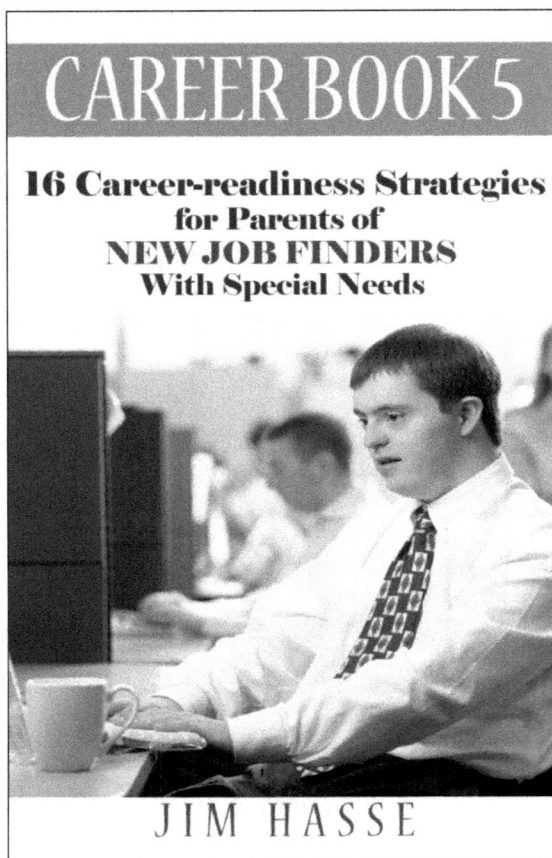

Buy **Career Book 5** on Amazon
at http://www.amazon.com/dp/B00KQRZIHC.

www.ingramcontent.com/pod-product-compliance
Lightning Source LLC
Chambersburg PA
CBHW060954040426
42445CB00011B/1152